T0055989

To access audio visit:
**www.halleonard.com/mylibrary**

Enter Code

4788-1918-0263-5767

Audio Arrangements by Peter Deneff

ISBN 978-1-61780-575-2

HAL•LEONARD®
CORPORATION
7777 W. BLUEMOUND RD. P.O. BOX 13819 MILWAUKEE, WI 53213

Visit Hal Leonard Online at
**www.halleonard.com**

# BACK TO DECEMBER

Words and Music by
TAYLOR SWIFT

TRUMPET

# BLANK SPACE

TRUMPET

Words and Music by TAYLOR SWIFT,
MAX MARTIN and SHELLBACK

To Coda ⊕

**D.S. al Coda**
**(take all repeats)**

**CODA** ⊕

*mf*

*f*

1.

2.

# FIFTEEN

TRUMPET

Words and Music by
TAYLOR SWIFT

# I KNEW YOU WERE TROUBLE

TRUMPET

Words and Music by TAYLOR SWIFT,
SHELLBACK and MAX MARTIN

# LOVE STORY

TRUMPET

Words and Music by
TAYLOR SWIFT

# MEAN

TRUMPET

Words and Music by
TAYLOR SWIFT

13

# OUR SONG

TRUMPET

Words and Music by
TAYLOR SWIFT

# PICTURE TO BURN

TRUMPET

Words and Music by TAYLOR SWIFT
and LIZ ROSE

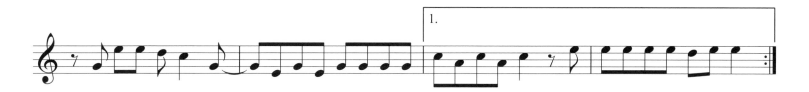

# SHAKE IT OFF

TRUMPET

Words and Music by TAYLOR SWIFT,
MAX MARTIN and SHELLBACK

D.S. al Coda

CODA

8

1.

2.

1.

2.

1.

2.

# SHOULD'VE SAID NO

TRUMPET

Words and Music by
TAYLOR SWIFT

# TEARDROPS ON MY GUITAR

TRUMPET

Words and Music by TAYLOR SWIFT
and LIZ ROSE

# 22

TRUMPET

Words and Music by TAYLOR SWIFT,
SHELLBACK and MAX MARTIN

# WE ARE NEVER EVER GETTING BACK TOGETHER

TRUMPET

Words and Music by TAYLOR SWIFT,
SHELLBACK and MAX MARTIN

**To Coda**

**D.S. al Coda**

**CODA**

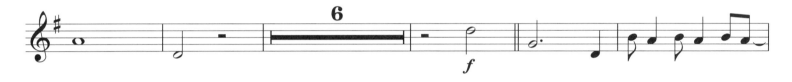

# WHITE HORSE

TRUMPET

Words and Music by TAYLOR SWIFT
and LIZ ROSE

# YOU BELONG WITH ME

Words and Music by TAYLOR SWIFT
and LIZ ROSE

TRUMPET